Lent and
*E*ASTER
*W*ISDOM
—— *from* ——
SAINT AUGUSTINE

Other Books in this Series from Liguori Publications

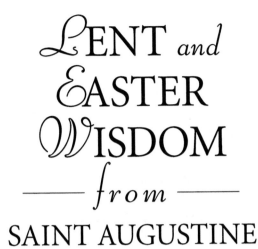

LENT and EASTER WISDOM from

SAINT AUGUSTINE

Daily Scripture and Prayers Together
With Saint Augustine's Own Words

Compiled by Agnes Cunningham, SSCM

Liguori
LIGUORI, MISSOURI

Imprimi Potest:
Harry Grile, CSsR, Provincial
Denver Province, The Redemptorists

Published by Liguori Publications, Liguori, Missouri 63057

To order, call 800-325-9521, or visit liguori.org

Copyright © 2013 Agnes Cunningham

Cataloging-in-Publication Data on file with the Library of Congress

p ISBN 978-07648-2031-1
e ISBN 978-07648-6935-3

The texts from St. Augustine that comprise the first section of each day featured in this book were gathered by and are the responsibility of the author, who obtained them from books listed on page 112.

Compliant with *The Roman Missal*, third edition.

Liguori Publications, a nonprofit corporation, is an apostolate of the Redemptorists. To learn more about the Redemptorists, visit Redemptorists.com.

Printed in the United States of America
17 16 15 14 13 / 5 4 3 2 1
First Edition

Contents

Introduction

Augustine of Hippo is one of the best known among the holy women and men honored as saints in the Roman Catholic Church. He is venerated by Christians and non-Christians alike. He has been quoted as an authority by Catholics as well as by those who oppose or reject the teachings of the Catholic Church. The story of his spiritual life has been called the most famous autobiography the world has known.

Augustine was born in 354 at Tagaste, in Northern Africa, to a devout Christian mother and a pagan father, who converted to Christianity shortly before his death. He had a brother, Navigius, and a sister whose name we do not know. She became the abbess of a convent in Hippo for which Augustine wrote many spiritual works.

Lack of money obliged Augustine to leave school at the age of sixteen, but he resumed studies one year later. That same year, he entered into a relationship with an unnamed young woman with whom he had a child. Though never married, the two lived in fidelity to each other until he was thirty-one years old. In his attempt to lead a life of chastity, he dismissed his mistress, but it would be only at the age of thirty-two that he fully embraced Christianity and was baptized by St. Ambrose.

Augustine's desire to live a monastic life in the company of a group of friends was brought to an end with his call to priesthood by popular acclaim in the church in Hippo. This was followed several years later by his becoming a bishop. He soon became recognized as an outstanding theologian, a learned anti-heretical writer, and a leading ecclesiastical statesman. During the thirty-four years of his episcopacy, he was a devoted pastor, giving himself wholeheartedly to the largely unlearned, simple people of his diocese.

Augustine's concern and affection for the people entrusted to his care are clearly reflected in the more than 500 extant sermons that still speak to us today. Their content reveals his knowledge of human nature, of his people as individuals, and of the experiences they encountered in the culture and practices of their daily lives. The insights, humor, and down-to-earth discourse of his sermons make them a primary source for the wisdom we seek as we journey through Lent and into Easter in this volume.

SR. AGNES CUNNINGHAM, SSCM

A Brief History of Lent

Most Catholics seem to be aware that the forty-day period before the solemnity of Easter—Lent, which comes from the Anglo-Saxon word *lencten*, meaning "spring"—is a time marked by particular rituals, such as the reception of ashes on Ash Wednesday or the decision to "give up French fries." Is Lent broader than just these practices that seem to be left over from another era?

In the first three centuries of Christian experience, preparation for the Easter feast usually covered a period of one or two days, perhaps a week at the most. St. Irenaeus of Lyons (ca. 140–202) even speaks of a forty-hour preparation for Easter.

The first reference to Lent as a period of forty days' preparation occurs in the teachings of the First Council of Nicaea in 325. By the end of the fourth century, a Lenten period of forty days was established and accepted.

In its early development, Lent quickly became associated with the sacrament of baptism, since Easter was the great baptismal feast. Those who were preparing to be baptized participated in the season of Lent in preparation for the reception of the sacrament of baptism. Eventually, those who were already baptized considered it important to join these candidates preparing for baptism in their preparations for Easter. The customs and practices of Lent as we know them today soon took hold.

LENT AS A JOURNEY

Lent is often portrayed as a journey, from one point in time to another. The concept of journey is obvious for those experiencing the Rite of Christian Initiation of Adults (RCIA), the program of baptismal preparation conducted in most parishes during Lent.

But Lenten preparation is not limited to those who are preparing to be baptized and join the Church. For many Catholics, Lent is a journey that is measured from Ash Wednesday through Easter Sunday, but more accurately Lent is measured from Ash Wednesday to the beginning of the period known as the Easter Triduum.

The Easter Triduum begins with the evening Mass of the Lord's Supper on Holy Thursday, reaches its high point in the Easter Vigil, and closes with Evening Prayer on Easter Sunday.

By whatever yardstick the journey is measured, it is not only the time that is important but the essential experiences of the journey that are necessary for a full appreciation of what is being celebrated.

The Lenten journey is also a process of spiritual growth and, as such, presumes movement from one state of being to another. For example, some people may find themselves troubled and anxious at the beginning of Lent as a result of a life choice or an unanswered question, and at the end of Lent, they may fully expect a sense of conversion, a sense of peace, or perhaps simply understanding and acceptance. Therefore, Lent is a movement from one point of view to another or, perhaps, from one interpretation of life to another.

Scripture, psalms, prayers, rituals, practices, and penance are the components of the Lenten journey. Each component, tried and tested by years of tradition, is one of the "engines" that drives the season and that brings the weary spiritual traveler to the joys of Easter.

PENITENTIAL NATURE OF LENT

A popular understanding of Lent is that it is a penitential period of time during which people attempt to become more sensitive to the role of sin in their lives. Lenten sermons will speak of personal sin, coming to an awareness of the sins of others and the effect such sin might have, and the sin that can be found within our larger society and culture. Awareness of sin, however, is balanced by an emphasis on the love and acceptance that God still has for humanity, despite the sinful condition in which we still find ourselves.

The practice of meditation on the passion of the Lord, his suffering, and his death is also seen as part of the penitential experience of Lent. There is also a traditional concern for the reception of the sacrament of reconciliation during Lent. Originally, the sacrament of reconciliation was celebrated before Lent began. The penance was imposed on Ash Wednesday and performed during the entire forty-day period.

SUMMONS TO PENITENTIAL LIVING

"Jesus came to Galilee proclaiming the gospel of God: 'This is the time of fulfillment. The kingdom of God is at hand. Repent, and believe in the gospel'" (Mark 1:14–15). This call to conversion announces the solemn opening of Lent. Participants are marked with ashes, and the words, "Repent, and believe in the Gospel," are prayed. This blessing is understood as a personal acceptance of the desire to take on the life of penance for the sake of the word of the Lord.

The example of Jesus in the desert for forty days—a time during which he fasted and prayed—is imitated. It is time to center attention on conversion. During Lent, the expectation is to examine our lives and, through the practice of prayer, fasting, and works of charity, seek to conform our lives to Christ's. For some, this conversion will be a turning from sin to grace. For others, it will be a gracious turning toward the mystery of God in Christ. Whatever the pattern chosen by a particular pilgrim for an observance of Lent, it is hoped that this book will provide a useful support in the effort.

PART I

~~~~~

READINGS
for
LENT

DAY 1

Journey Together

*C*hristians ought to be fervently engaged in almsgiving and fasting and prayer throughout their lives; much more so then at the approach of the great festival of Easter, which rouses our minds as it comes round again each year renewing in them the salutary memory of what mercy our Lord, the only Son of God, has bestowed on us, of how he fasted and prayed for us....What greater mercy, though, could there be toward the miserable, than that which pulled the Creator down from heaven and clothed the founder of the earth in an earthly body?

SERMON 207, I

SCRIPTURE

Have among yourselves the same attitude that is also yours in Christ Jesus, Who, though he was in the form of God, did not regard equality with God something to be grasped. Rather, he emptied himself, taking the form of a slave, coming in human likeness; and found human in appearance, he humbled himself, becoming obedient to death, even death on a cross. Because of this, God greatly exalted him and bestowed on him the name that is above every name, that at the name of Jesus every knee should bend, of those in heaven and on earth and under the earth, and every tongue confess that Jesus Christ is Lord, to the glory of God the Father.

PHILIPPIANS 2:5–11

PRAYER

Lord Jesus Christ, today we begin—you and I—a journey together along the path that leads to Calvary and death. I feel overwhelmed at the thought of what I have decided to undertake, but I know that I am not alone. As you commit yourself to do the Father's will, so do I commit myself as a disciple who longs to be faithful to your call. With you I say, "Father, not my will, but thine, be done." Amen.

PRACTICE

Wear the ashes you receive today as a witness to your resolve to spend this holy season as a time to grow in faith and love through prayer, fasting, and charity to the poor and the abandoned.

DAY 2

Fasting From Vanity, Feasting on Promise

*B*y fasting for forty days before his death in the flesh, it's as though Jesus was crying out, "Hold yourselves in check from the desires of this world"; while by eating and drinking for forty days after his resurrection in the flesh it's as though he was crying out, *Behold I am with you until the consummation of the world....*While we are traveling the way of the Lord, you see, we should at one and the same time be fasting from the vanity of the present age, and feasting on the promise of the age to come; not setting our hearts on this one, feeding our hearts lifted up to that one.

SERMON 263A

SCRIPTURE

I give you thanks, Lord and King, I praise you, God my savior! I declare your name, refuge of my life, because you have ransomed my life from death; You held back my body from the pit, and delivered my foot from the power of Sheol....You have rescued me according to your abundant mercy from the snare of those who look for my downfall, and from the power of those who seek my life. From many dangers you have saved me...from deceiving lips and painters of lies, from the arrows of a treacherous tongue.

SIRACH 51:1–2, 3, 5–6

PRAYER

Loving Lord Jesus, today I want to reflect on the mystery of my baptism and, through it, my entrance into the mystery of your death and resurrection. As I move through the days of this holy season, may I be open to the grace that leads to the renewal of my baptismal vows, with a deeper commitment to the life of discipleship that they call for as I seek to follow you in divine freedom and truth. Amen.

PRACTICE

Take time to pray for the priest who administered the sacrament of baptism to you and for those faithful friends who agreed to be your sponsors in the Christian life.

DAY 3

Learn Something

*I*t is the task of Christians daily to make progress toward God, and always to rejoice in God or in his gifts. For the time of our pilgrimage, our wandering in exile, is extremely short, and in our home country time does not exist....This is a school in which God is the only teacher, and it demands good students, ones who are keen in attendance, not ones who play truant....We learn something from commandments, something from examples, something from sacraments. These things are remedies for our wounds, material for our studies.

SERMON 16A, I

SCRIPTURE

Those live whom the LORD protects; yours is the life of my spirit. You have given me health and restored my life! Peace in place of bitterness! You have preserved my life from the pit of destruction; behind your back you cast all my sins. For it is not Sheol that gives you thanks, nor death that praises you.... Parents declare to their children, O God, your faithfulness. The LORD is there to save us. We shall play our music in the house of the LORD all the days of our life.

ISAIAH 38:16–18, 19–20

PRAYER

Loving Father, send your Holy Spirit, the Spirit of truth and light, into our minds to remove from the eyes of our heart the darkness and blindness that prevent us from seeing the errors of our ways, the sinfulness that lurks in our souls. May each Friday in Lent, with its invitation to abstinence, lead us to recognize what it is we must renounce so as to live as true members of your divine Son. Amen.

PRACTICE

Today, identify something other than the food from which you abstain and offer it to God for your spiritual health.

DAY 4

SATURDAY AFTER ASH WEDNESDAY

Believe in Christ

*T*he medicine for all the wounds of the soul, and the one way of atoning for all human delinquency, is to believe in Christ; nor is it in the least possible for any people to be cleansed, either of original sin which they have contracted from Adam, in whom all have sinned, and become children of wrath by nature, or of the sins which they have added themselves....By believing in him they become children of God, because they are born of God adoptively by the grace which consists of faith in Jesus Christ our Lord.

SERMON 143, I

SCRIPTURE

For those who are led by the Spirit of God are children of God. For you did not receive a spirit of slavery to fall back into fear, but you received a spirit of adoption, through which we cry, "Abba, Father!" The Spirit itself bears witness with our spirit that we are children of God, and if children, then heirs, heirs of God and joint heirs with Christ, if only we suffer with him so that we may also be glorified with him.

ROMANS 8:15–17

PRAYER

Gracious God, give us the grace to recognize the treasures of the family to which we belong as your adopted children: blessed to be cherished members of Jesus Christ, daughters and sons of the Blessed Virgin Mary. We are wealthy in the inheritance that is ours through the communion of all the saints, destined for that country where we hope to live with you in the heavenly homeland that has been won for us through your Son. Amen.

PRACTICE

Pray for the conversion of sinners who fail to recognize the love of God that surrounds them and desires only their good in this life and for all eternity.

FIRST SUNDAY OF LENT

Make Many Offerings

*J*t's not enough to change one's behavior for the better, and to give up bad activities, unless for things you have already done you also make it up to God by the sorrow of repentance, by the groans of humility, by the sacrifice of a contrite heart, with almsgiving thrown in to help you along. *Blessed*, you see, *are the merciful, since God will have mercy on them*....And the humility with which one humbles oneself before the Church of God is much more honorable; and a much lighter labor is imposed, and without any risk at all of temporal death, eternal death is avoided.

SERMON 351, 12

SCRIPTURE

To keep the law is to make many offerings; whoever observes the commandments sacrifices a peace offering. By works of charity one offers fine flour, and one who gives alms presents a sacrifice of praise. To refrain from evil pleases the Lord, and to avoid injustice is atonement.

SIRACH 35:1–5

PRAYER

Gracious Father, with the wonderful freedom of the children of God, you have given us the gift of being able to choose the way in which we express to you our love, our worship, and our repentance for our sins and failings. We resolve to live in response to the call of your beloved Son to be his disciples. Give us the light of your Holy Spirit to see clearly what it is we are to do to fulfill your will. Amen.

PRACTICE

In your efforts to develop a relationship of peace and harmony, be gentle today in dealing with someone you know who seems to make life difficult for you.

DAY 6

Return to the Lord

You mustn't regard fasting as an unimportant or superfluous matter. Please don't think to yourself, when perhaps you are fasting because it is the Church's custom, don't say to yourself, or listen to the suggestions of the tempter inside you, saying, "What are you doing, you and your fasting? You're cheating your soul, you're not giving it what it takes delight in. You're inflicting punishment on yourself, you have turned into your own torturer and executioner. So does your torturing yourself please God? That means he's cruel, if he enjoys your being punished." Answer this sort of tempter like this: "Yes, I do hurt myself, so that he may spare me."

SERMON 400, 3

SCRIPTURE

Yet even now—oracle of the LORD—return to me with your whole heart, with fasting, weeping, and mourning. Rend your hearts, not your garments, and return to the LORD, your God, for he is gracious and merciful, slow to anger, abounding in steadfast love, and relenting in punishment...."Spare your people, LORD! Do not let your heritage become a disgrace, a byword among the nations! Why should they say among the peoples, 'Where is their God?'"

JOEL 2:12–13, 17

PRAYER

Dear loving Father, how often people picture you as a stern, rigorous judge who desires only the submission of our wills in every area of our lives. Help me to remember the beautiful lessons your Son, Jesus, taught his followers about a Father who is kind and merciful, ready to forgive, and ever present to support us in the trials and sufferings of life. Amen.

PRACTICE

Share with someone you know your conviction about the infinite mercy of God, a Father whom we can know and love and whose bountiful graces are always ready to assist us in our needs.

DAY 7

Prayer Seeks Peace

*D*uring these days you restrain your desires for lawful things; it's in order not to commit unlawful things. In this way, in humility and charity, by fasting and giving, by restraining ourselves and pardoning, by paying out good deeds and not paying back bad ones, by turning away from evil and doing good, our prayer seeks peace and obtains it. Prayer, you see, flies beautifully when it's supported on wings of such virtues and is in this way more readily wafted through to heaven, where Christ our peace has preceded us.

SERMON 206, 3

SCRIPTURE

Is this the manner of fasting I would choose, a day to afflict oneself? To bow one's head like a reed, and lie upon sackcloth and ashes? Is this what you call a fast, a day acceptable to the LORD? *Is this not, rather, the fast that I choose: releasing those bound unjustly, untying the thongs of the yoke; setting free the oppressed, breaking off every yoke? Is it not sharing your bread with the hungry, bringing the afflicted and the homeless into your house; clothing the naked when you see them, and not turning your back on your own flesh? Then your light shall break forth like the dawn...and your gloom shall become like midday.*

ISAIAH 58:5–8, 10

PRAYER

Lord Jesus Christ, you have called us to a way of life that honors prayer, fasting, and the giving of alms. You have also widened the horizons of our minds and opened our eyes to the realities of life in this world. As we recognize the suffering of people among whom we live, we pray for the grace to know how to bring support to those less fortunate than we and always to be generous in what we share. Amen.

PRACTICE

Look among your "treasures" and choose something you think you cannot live without and offer it to someone to whom it will bring joy.

DAY 8

Our Common Condition

*A*lmsgiving, which is not to be made light of, is bestowed on any poor people by right of humanity, seeing that the Lord himself relieved the wants of the poor....So then, we are not to support sinners, precisely insofar as they are sinners; and yet because they are also human beings, we must treat them too with humane consideration. Let us relentlessly pursue their own wickedness in them, while showing mercy to their and our common condition. And in this way, *let us be tireless, while we have the time, in doing good to all, though supremely to those at home in the faith.*

SERMON 164A, 4

SCRIPTURE

Good and upright is the LORD,
  therefore he shows sinners the way,
He guides the humble in righteousness,
  and teaches the humble his way.
All the paths of the LORD are mercy and truth
  toward those who honor his covenant and decrees....
Who is the one who fears the LORD?
  God shows him the way he should choose.
He will abide in prosperity,
  and his descendants will inherit the land.

PSALM 25:8–10, 12–13

PRAYER

Lord Jesus, you gave your life to save us from the burden of sin that rested so heavily on the entire human race. Help us to believe in your great love for us, for all those who struggle against the wiles of the Evil One and the enticements of temptation in their daily lives. Gentle Son of God, have mercy on me, but above all, strengthen my faith and trust in you, my Lord and my God! Amen.

PRACTICE

Spend some time in prayer, asking for the grace of repentance for the sins of your life and the courage to live faithful to the word of God.

DAY 9

Take Careful Stock of Your Charity

*S*ubmit yourselves to a thorough interrogation, turn out your innermost closets and cupboards. Take careful stock of how much you have of charity—and increase the stock you find. Pay attention to that sort of treasure so that you may be rich within. Other things that carry a high price tag are said to be dear, aren't they—and quite rightly. Look at the way you normally talk: "This is dearer than that." What do you mean by "it's dearer" but that it has a higher price—it's more precious. Now, if whatever is more precious is said to be dearer, what can be dearer than dearness itself, which is what charity means?

SERMON 34, 7

SCRIPTURE

Do not appear before the Lord empty-handed, for all that you offer is in fulfillment of the precepts. The offering of the just enriches the altar: a sweet odor before the Most High. The sacrifice of the just is accepted, never to be forgotten. With a generous spirit pay homage to the Lord, and do not spare your freewill gifts....Give to the Most High as he has given to you, generously, according to your means. For he is a God who always repays and will give back to you sevenfold.

SIRACH 35:6–10, 12–13

PRAYER

Loving Father, how can I measure the abundance of gifts you have bestowed on me since the beginning of my life? Gifts of nature and of grace, the treasure of your beloved Son, the overwhelming benefits that have come into my life through so many people who have loved and nourished me and encouraged me to keep your Commandments, and the open door of your heart when I return to you after straying. Teach me to be grateful and faithful. Amen.

PRACTICE

Spend the day in repentance of heart for your failure to love our gracious, generous God, who desires to be a merciful Father to you.

DAY 10

FRIDAY OF THE FIRST WEEK OF LENT

Let the One Who Has...

*R*emember the poor, so that what you withhold from your-selves by living more sparingly, you may deposit in the treasury of heaven. Let the hungry Christ receive what the fasting Christian receives less of. Let the self-denial of one who undertakes it willingly become the support of the one who has nothing. Let the voluntary want of the person who has plenty become the needed plenty of the person in want. Again, let there be in mild-mannered and humble spirits a compassionate ease in forgiving. Let the one who has done an injury ask pardon; let the one who has suffered an injury grant pardon; so that we may not be possessed by Satan.

SERMON 210, 12

SCRIPTURE

Therefore, putting away falsehood, speak the truth, each one to his neighbor, for we are members one of another. Be angry but do not sin; do not let the sun set on your anger, and do not leave room for the devil....And do not grieve the holy Spirit of God, with which you were sealed for the day of redemption. All bitterness, fury, anger, shouting, and reviling, must be removed from you, along with all malice. [And] be kind to one another, compassionate, forgiving one another as God has forgiven you in Christ.

EPHESIANS 4:25–27, 30–32

PRAYER

Gentle heart of Jesus, grant me the grace to live the gentle life, seeking only to spread peace and harmony, understanding and kindness to those around me, especially those with whom I live and work. Let me be an agent of peace, a messenger of reconciliation, bringing understanding and pardon where there is anger and bitterness. Let your goodness shine through me to others. Let me truly live the beatitude of those who are children of God because they are peacemakers. Amen.

PRACTICE

Do an act of kindness today for someone who is experiencing feelings of rejection and isolation from family members or colleagues in the workplace.

DAY 11

For in You Has My Soul Put Its Trust

In both the good things and the bad things of this world, in all of them temptation is to be met. So...the Christian is never wholly safe. He must say...with his whole heart...: *Have mercy on me, Lord, have mercy on me, for in you has my soul put its trust....*No one at all, you see, whose soul has put its trust in God is either made overconfident by good fortune or broken by bad. Such people know that all these things pass like a shadow, but that he doesn't pass to whom they have said, *In you has my soul put its trust.*

SERMON 20A, I

SCRIPTURE

Blessed is the man who perseveres in temptation, for when he has been proved he will receive the crown of life that he promised to those who love him. No one experiencing temptation should say, "I am being tempted by God"; for God is not subject to temptation to evil, and he himself tempts no one. Rather, each person is tempted when he is lured and enticed by his own desire. Then desire conceives and brings forth sin, and when sin reaches maturity it gives birth to death. Do not be deceived, my beloved...: all good giving and every perfect gift is from above, coming down from the Father of lights, with whom there is no alteration or shadow caused by change.

JAMES 1:12–17

PRAYER

Dear God, I truly believe that "every perfect gift comes down" from you, the Father of lights and the God of all consolation. Let me not cease to cherish your goodness, your superabundant generosity, and your will to love me always more than I could ever love myself. Let me seek to show this prodigality to those I know, as I seek to alleviate the suffering of those around me and reach out in understanding to all. Amen.

PRACTICE

Today, take a deliberate stand to step aside from something that might give you pleasure so that it may be offered and given to someone else.

DAY 12

THE SECOND SUNDAY OF LENT

Offer a Prayer

What calls for all our efforts in this life is the healing of the eyes of our hearts, with which God is to be seen. It is for this that the holy mysteries are celebrated, for this that the Word of God is preached, to this that the Church's moral exhortations are directed....Whatever points are made by God's holy Scriptures, this is their ultimate point, to help us purge that inner faculty of ours from that thing that prevents us from beholding God....The eye of the heart, when it is unsettled and hurt, turns itself away from the light of justice, and neither dares nor is able to gaze upon it.

SERMON 88, 5

SCRIPTURE

Hear Lord, my plea for justice; pay heed to my cry;
Listen to my prayer from lips without guile.
From you let my vindication come; your eyes see what is right.
You have tested my heart, searched it in the night.
You have tried me by fire, but find no malice in me.
My mouth has not transgressed as others often do.
As your lips have instructed me,
I have kept from the way of the lawless.
My steps have kept to your paths; my feet have not faltered.

PSALM 17:1–5

PRAYER

Lord, as I make my defense before the throne of your mercy, let me not speak in arrogance or blindness of heart. If the just person sins seven times a day, what must I say of myself? Let me confess my failings in simplicity and truth, knowing that forgiveness is offered by your beloved Son seventy times seven. Amen.

PRACTICE

Offer a prayer for someone who is unable to trust in the mercy and goodness of God, who wills only that the sinner believe, repent, and live.

DAY 13

Our Daily Purification Is the Lord's Prayer

*T*hrough Christ and in Christ, I implore you, abound in good works, in kindness, in goodness, in generosity. Be quick to forgive wrongs done to you. None of you must nurse your anger against another or you will be blocking your prayer to God.... Sins, after all, are not just those that are called serious offenses.... To pay attention to something you ought not to is a sin; to listen to something willingly which shouldn't have been listened to is a sin; to think something that shouldn't have been thought is a sin. But our Lord has given us other remedies for every day....Our daily purification is the Lord's Prayer.

SERMON 261, 9

SCRIPTURE

So be imitators of God, as beloved children, and live in love, as Christ loved us and handed himself over for us as a sacrificial offering to God for a fragrant aroma. Immorality or any impurity or greed must not even be mentioned among you, as is fitting among holy ones, no obscenity or silly or suggestive talk, which is out of place, but instead, thanksgiving....For you were once darkness, but now you are light in the Lord. Live as children of light.

EPHESIANS 5:1–4, 8

PRAYER

Father in heaven, your Son, Jesus, taught us that the way to learn how to pray is to turn to you in words that he himself taught us. May your kingdom come in our lives; may your will be done in our actions; may your name be hallowed in our words. Let us, through the grace of the Holy Spirit whom you and your Son have sent to us, become a living song of praise to your glory. Amen.

PRACTICE

Offer an act of sacrifice today for someone who struggles to think of God as a Father who wills only the return of the sinner from wayward ways and fullness of life in his love.

DAY 14

TUESDAY OF THE SECOND WEEK OF LENT

Be Angry and Do Not Sin

*W*hat is repentance, after all, but being angry with oneself? What's the idea of beating your breast if you aren't just pretending? Why beat it if you aren't angry with it? So when you beat your breast, you are being angry with your heart in order to make amends to your Lord. This is also how we can understand the text, "Be angry and do not sin." ...Be angry because you have sinned, and by punishing yourself, stop sinning. Give your heart a shaking by repentance, and this will be a sacrifice to God.

SERMON 19, 2

SCRIPTURE

Come now, let us set things right, says the LORD: Though your sins be like scarlet, they may become white as snow; Though they be red like crimson, they may become white as wool. If you are willing, and obey, you shall eat the good things of the land; But if you refuse and resist, you shall be eaten by the sword: for the mouth of the LORD has spoken! ...Zion shall be redeemed by justice, and her repentant ones by righteousness.

ISAIAH 1:18–20, 27

PRAYER

Heavenly Father, so many people seem to be burdened by memories of growing up as Catholics in a Church that taught only the dark side of the Gospel. Today, I pray for these people, because I have been blessed in my life with the graces of a different experience. I have known a loving God, a Church that is truly a mother to us all, a Gospel of peace and benediction. Thank you for these gifts that I ask to share with everyone I know. Amen.

PRACTICE

Strive in such a way today that everyone you meet will be drawn to the Lord, who gives joy to your heart and peace to your soul.

DAY 15

Let Charity Be Exercised
by Living Good Lives

*T*he heedless person forgets to put an end to a quarrel; the stubborn one is loath to grant pardon when asked; the person who is proudly ashamed disdains to beg pardon. Animosities live on in these three vices, but they kill the soul in which they don't die. Let a spirit of recollection keep watch against heedlessness, of compassion against vindictive stubbornness, of gentle good sense against proud shame....Let charity be exercised by your living good lives; while insofar as there is little of it there, let it be obtained by your praying for it.

SERMON 209, I

SCRIPTURE

Know this, [beloved]: everyone should be quick to hear, slow to speak, slow to wrath, for the wrath of a man does not accomplish the righteousness of God. Therefore, put away all filth and evil excess and humbly welcome the word that has been planted in you and is able to save your souls. Be doers of the word and not hearers only, deluding yourselves. For if anyone is a hearer of the word and not a doer, he is like a man who looks at his own face in a mirror. He sees himself, then goes off and promptly forgets what he looked like. But the one who peers into the perfect law of freedom and perseveres, and is not a hearer who forgets but a doer who acts, such a one shall be blessed in what he does.

JAMES 1:19–25

PRAYER

Dear Lord, how rarely we remember the lessons we learned in our childhood about your Father and his goodness and love for all his daughters and sons. Today, I reflect on the seven deadly sins, grateful for the grace that has enabled me to resist the snares of the Evil One and recognize the goodness that has protected me throughout my life. Thank you for the saints and angels who care for me, watch over me, and never cease to inspire me to be faithful to you. Amen.

PRACTICE

Call on the treasury of the communion of saints to face a spiritual challenge that is a burden in your life at this time.

THURSDAY OF THE SECOND WEEK OF LENT

Wake Him Up

*C*hristian, Christ is asleep in your boat; wake him up, he will command the storm, and everything will be calm. At that time ...when the disciples were being tossed about in the boat and Christ was asleep, they represented Christians being tossed about while their Christian faith is asleep....What does it mean, faith is asleep? It has been drugged. What does that mean, it has been drugged? You have forgotten it. So what does it mean, to wake up Christ? Waking up your faith, remembering what you have believed. So then, recall your faith, wake up Christ; your very faith will command the waves. They will fade away immediately, immediately everything will grow calm.

SERMON 361, 7

SCRIPTURE

No evil can harm the one who fears the LORD; through trials, again and again he is rescued. Whoever hates the law is without wisdom, and is tossed about like a boat in a storm. The prudent trust in the word of the LORD, and the law is dependable for them as a divine oracle....Like clay in the hands of a potter, to be molded according to his pleasure, so are people in the hands of their Maker, to be dealt with as he decides. As evil contrasts with good, and death with life, so are sinners in contrast with the godly....Since by the Lord's blessing I have made progress till like a grape-picker I have filled my wine press, consider that not for myself only have I labored, but for all who seek instruction.

SIRACH 33:1–3, 13–14, 17–18

PRAYER

Great God of my life, as the years go on, it seems to become increasingly difficult to live a life of faith. I come to confess my belief in you and in the fullness of the revelation you have made known to us in your beloved Son, Jesus Christ. Lord, I do believe. Strengthen my faith. Let me not be led astray by the intricate and specious arguments of this world's thoughts, but turn always to you for light and guidance in all things. Amen.

PRACTICE

Say the Lord's Prayer today as an act of faith in the God whom Jesus has taught us to call "Abba."

DAY 17

Now It's Time for Faith

*L*et us all have the good sense to heed the warnings of our instructor, and so not waste the time of the mercy of our savior, which is being spread out for us now, as long as the human race is being spared. The reason, you see, we are being spared is so that we may be converted, and there may be no one to be condemned. God knows, of course, when the end of the world is to come; now, however, it's the time for faith. Whether the end of the world will find any of us still here, I don't know; and perhaps it won't.

SERMON 109, I

SCRIPTURE

Lord, you have been our refuge through all generations.
Before the mountains were born,
the earth and the world brought forth,
from eternity to eternity you are God.
You turn humanity back into dust,
saying, "Return, you children of Adam!"
A thousand years in your eyes are merely a day gone by,
Before a watch passes in the night, you wash them away;
They sleep,
and in the morning they sprout again like an herb....
Teach us to count our days aright,
that we may gain wisdom of heart.

PSALM 90:1–5, 12

PRAYER

Come, Holy Spirit, Spirit of God, Spirit of Jesus! Come with your sevenfold gift to guide us along the way of our Lenten journey. Through you, we are enabled to grow in knowledge of our loving Father, to grow daily in likeness to Jesus Christ, and to live enlightened by holy wisdom. We pray for the grace to be submissive to your guidance, for you are the source of light and love. We give thanks for your presence in our lives. Amen.

PRACTICE

Be open to the inspiration of the Holy Spirit, however and wherever it may come to you, and follow the Spirit's guidance along the pathway to peace.

DAY 18

Ask, Seek, Knock

*A*sk, seek, knock, you will receive, you will find, the door will be opened to you. Only don't just ask, seek, and knock with your voices, but also with your morals; do good works, without which you certainly have no business to lead this life. Wipe out your sins by daily good works. Not even slight sins are to be treated lightly. They are nothing very big, of course; but they do pile up, they make a heap; they pile up and make a lump....Those tiny sins, without which human life cannot be lived, trickle in little by little. Don't let your hands rest, I'm saying, but from good works.

SERMON 77B, 7

SCRIPTURE

Ask and it will be given to you; seek and you will find; knock and the door will be opened to you. For everyone who asks, receives; and the one who seeks, finds; and to the one who knocks, the door will be opened. Which one of you would hand his son a stone when he asks for a loaf of bread, or a snake when he asks for a fish? If you then, who are wicked, know how to give good gifts to your children, how much more will your heavenly Father give good things to those who ask him.

MATTHEW 7:7–11

PRAYER

Lord Jesus, you encourage us to be perfect, as our heavenly Father is perfect. This is a goal that lies beyond my ability to attain. But you have promised to be with us, to teach us the way of truth, to dwell in us with your Father if we open our hearts in love to those in need. Today, I ask for the graces you have promised so that I can answer, "Yes!" to every call I hear from you. Amen.

PRACTICE

Try to live in such a way that you may radiate the tenderness of Christ to everyone you meet.

DAY 19

Like Meets Like

*B*e grains of wheat. There are masses of chaff on the threshing floor, but the winnowing is going to come, the chaff will be separated, and not a single wisp of it enters the granary with you, not a single grain goes on the fire....Keep an eye out for the good people to imitate; be good yourselves, and you'll find them....You will find good Christians, believe me; good married men being faithful to their wives; good married women being faithful to their husbands. Seek and you will find; be good yourselves and it won't escape your notice. Like meets like.

SERMON 260D, 2

SCRIPTURE

Amen, amen, I say to you, unless a grain of wheat falls to the ground and dies, it remains just a grain of wheat; but if it dies, it produces much fruit. Whoever loves his life loses it, and whoever hates his life in this world will preserve it for eternal life. Whoever serves me must follow me, and where I am, there also will my servant be. The Father will honor whoever serves me.

JOHN 12:24–26

PRAYER

Gracious and loving God, your Son, Jesus, has told us about wheat. Perhaps this symbol is most meaningful because of its use for the fulfillment of his promise to be with us always until the end of time in the Real Presence of the Eucharist. The many grains that come together to make one loaf remind us of our call to one faith, one Lord, one baptism. It is for this I pray. Amen.

PRACTICE

Spend some time today in the presence of the Blessed Sacrament in gratitude for the gracious providence of God toward those who hunger for food and for the bread that gives life to our souls.

DAY 20

MONDAY OF THE THIRD WEEK OF LENT

A Way for Us

*I*n this life we are still wandering exiles, still sighing in faith for I know not what kind of home country. And why "I know not what kind," seeing that we are its citizens unless it is because by wandering away into a far country we have forgotten our true native land, and so can say about it, "I know not what kind of place it is." This amnesia is driven from our hearts by the Lord Christ, king of that country, as he comes to join us in our exile; and by his taking of flesh, his divinity becomes a way for us.

SERMON 362, 4

SCRIPTURE

Beloved, I urge you as aliens and sojourners to keep away from worldly desires that wage war against the soul. Maintain good conduct among the Gentiles, so that if they speak of you as evildoers, they may observe your good works and glorify God on the day of visitation. Be subject to every human institution for the Lord's sake, whether it be to the king as supreme or to governors as sent by him for the punishment of evildoers and the approval of those who do good. For it is the will of God that by doing good you may silence the ignorance of foolish people. Be free, yet without using freedom as a pretext for evil, but as slaves of God. Give honor to all, love the community, fear God, honor the king.

1 PETER 2:11–17

PRAYER

Lord Jesus Christ, how true it is that I may be the only Gospel proclaimed by my life to some people in this world. Like St. Francis of Assisi, help me to understand that it is not always necessary to use words to share your message. Help me to live so that I may be a living proclamation of that kingdom you proclaimed, the kingdom of your Father, to which we are all called. Amen.

PRACTICE

Take time today to read from one of the Gospels, asking for the grace to be ever more faithful to the inspiration that comes from the life and teachings of Jesus.

DAY 21

Put It All Down to Grace

*B*eware, O Christian, beware of pride. You may well be an imitator of the saints, but always put it all down to grace, because that you should be something left over is the work of God's grace in you, not of your own merits....Don't start getting swollen-headed about your merits; otherwise grace is no longer grace.... So put it entirely down to his loving kindness that you are just.... Because every crime, misdeed, or sin comes from our negligence, and all virtue and sanctity comes from God's indulgence.

SERMON 100, 4

SCRIPTURE

Consider your own calling, [beloved]. Not many of you were wise by human standards, not many were powerful, not many were of noble birth. Rather, God chose the foolish of the world to shame the wise, and God chose the weak of the world to shame the strong, and God chose the lowly and despised of the world, those who count for nothing, to reduce to nothing those who are something, so that no human being might boast before God. It is due to him that you are in Christ Jesus, who became for us wisdom from God, as well as righteousness, sanctification, and redemption, so that, as it is written, "Whoever boasts, should boast in the Lord."

1 CORINTHIANS 1:26–31

PRAYER

Abba, Father God, let me understand that I must learn to boast in the cross of our Lord Jesus Christ and count my worth, not in earthly possessions or heritage, but in the glory that is mine as your loved, adopted child. This is the inheritance and the honor that I choose to cherish. Grant that I may live so as to be worthy of the gift you have bestowed on me. Amen.

PRACTICE

Ask for the gift of humility of heart, surrendering yourself to God's will in all that happens to you today.

DAY 22

Resist the Temptation

When the Lord had been tempted with the triple temptation—because in all the allurements of the world these
three are to be found, either pleasure or curiosity or pride—what
did the evangelist say? *After the devil had concluded every temptation;*
every kind but of the alluring sort. There remained the other sort
of temptation, by harsh and hard treatment; yes, there remained
the other sort of temptation....He will return; he will enter into
Judas, he will make him betray his master; he will bring along the
Jews, not flattering now, but raging; taking possession of his own
instruments he will cry out with the tongues of all of them, *Crucify
him, crucify him!*

SERMON 284, 5

SCRIPTURE

Then an argument broke out among them about which of them should be regarded as the greatest. He said to them, "The kings of the Gentiles lord it over them and those in authority over them are addressed as 'Benefactors'; but among you it shall not be so. Rather, let the greatest among you be as the youngest, and the leader as the servant....I am among you as the one who serves. It is you who have stood by me in my trials; and I confer a kingdom on you, just as my Father has conferred one on me, that you may eat and drink at my table in my kingdom; and you will sit on thrones judging the twelve tribes of Israel."

LUKE 22:24–30

PRAYER

Lord Jesus Christ, you came into the world to fulfill the Father's will. King of the nations, you became a humble servant to show us how to serve one another. Grant me the grace to resist the temptation to claim the first place in an assembly, to impose my preferences because of the esteem I claim is due to me. Help me to remember that everything I have is given to serve you and give glory to your Father. Amen.

PRACTICE

Look for occasions to offer simple services to the persons with whom you live and work, in the spirit of Jesus, the servant of God.

DAY 23

Christ Humbled Himself

*T*he Lord Christ humbled himself, so that we might know how to be humble. Though containing all things he was conceived; though giving birth to all things he was born; though giving life to all things he died; but after three days he rose again, and ascended into heaven, and placed the human flesh which he had taken to himself at the Father's right hand....Which is the harder to believe, that God did such things, or that the world was able to believe them? Which indeed, particularly if we consider the way in which the world believed.

SERMON 272A

SCRIPTURE

Who would believe what we have heard? To whom has the arm of the LORD been revealed? He grew up like a sapling before him, like a shoot from the parched earth; he had no majestic bearing to catch our eye, no beauty to draw us to him....Yet it was our pain that he bore, our sufferings he endured. We thought of him as stricken, struck down by God and afflicted, but he was pierced for our sins, crushed for our iniquity. He bore the punishment that makes us whole, by his wounds we were healed.

ISAIAH 53:1–2, 4–5

PRAYER

Merciful Father, your beloved Son, Jesus, was perhaps nowhere more humble than in the suffering he took upon himself to atone for our sins and bring salvation to the world. The startling reality of the passion and suffering of our dear Savior is too much for our human minds to grasp. We turn to his holy Mother, Mary, who walked the way to Calvary with him, as we ask for the grace to share with her to the best of our ability. Amen.

PRACTICE

Spend some time today with Mary in contemplating the sorrows and rejection of her Son, Jesus, as he offers himself as a sacrifice for our salvation.

DAY 24

Do Not Neglect Hospitality

What a mystery, my brothers and sisters!...Learn to take in strangers as guests, where Christ can be recognized. Or didn't you know that if you take in any Christian, you are taking in him? Didn't he say himself, *I was a stranger, and you took me in?*... So when a Christian takes in a Christian, members are serving members; and the head rejoices, and reckons as given to himself whatever has been lavished on a member of his.

SERMON 236, 3

SCRIPTURE

Let mutual love continue. Do not neglect hospitality, for through it some have unknowingly entertained angels. Be mindful of prisoners as if sharing their imprisonment, and of the ill-treated as of yourselves, for you also are in the body. Let marriage be honored among all and the marriage bed be kept undefiled, for God will judge the immoral and adulterers. Let your life be free from love of money but be content with what you have, for he has said, "I will never forsake you or abandon you." Thus we may say with confidence: "The Lord is my helper, [and] I will not be afraid. What can anyone do to me?"

HEBREWS 13:1–6

PRAYER

Dear Jesus, today, as I find myself walking with you on the journey to Calvary, I pray that my search to know God's purpose in my life may be expressed in the silence I keep before every false accusation that may be leveled against me, whether the matter be great or small. As you were condemned to death, so let me affirm the life you bring to all those you call your own, the life I treasure as your gift to me. Amen.

PRACTICE

Reflect today on the First Station of the Cross, where Jesus is condemned to death before the tribunal of Pilate.

DAY 25

Live Patiently

As long as we are living here, however fortunate our circumstances, let us live patiently. Now all of us, or almost all of us, are afraid of dying. Sickness may befall us, or it may not. The loss of our dear ones is something we fear; it's possible we may lose them, it's possible we won't. Whatever bad thing you may fear on this earth, it may possibly happen, it may possibly not. Death cannot possibly not happen. It can be delayed, it can't be eliminated. And yet everybody works so hard to put off the evil day....The reason people toil away is not in order not to die, but just in order to die a little later.

SERMON 359A, 8

SCRIPTURE

Are you unaware that we who were baptized into Christ Jesus were baptized into his death? We were indeed buried with him through baptism into death, so that, just as Christ was raised from the dead by the glory of the Father, we too might live in newness of life. For if we have grown into union with him through a death like his, we shall also be united with him in the resurrection....If, then, we have died with Christ, we believe that we shall also live with him....As to his death, he died to sin once and for all; as to his life, he lives for God. Consequently, you too must think of yourselves as [being] dead to sin and living for God in Christ Jesus.

ROMANS 6:3–5, 8, 10–11

PRAYER

Just Father, your beloved Son was made to take up the cross placed on his shoulders by the Roman soldiers who had scourged and mocked him at Pilate's command. The thought of carrying it along the rugged way to Calvary is beyond my imagination. How often do I reach out, at least in my prayers if in no other way, to comfort and support those who are the victims of human cruelty? Let me never grow insensitive or deaf to the cries of the poor. Amen.

PRACTICE

Reflect on the pain that is uniquely yours and ask for the grace to be humble and gentle of heart under its burden.

DAY 26

Practice Kindness

*K*indness, my brothers and sisters...kindness is what you must practice, because sins abound. There is no other relief, no other road by which we can reach God, by which we can be made whole, be reconciled to him, whom we have so dangerously offended. We are going to come into his presence; may our works speak up for us there—and so speak up that they outweigh our offenses. You see, it's the side that's heavier that will gain the day, either for punishment if our sins deserve it or for relief and rest if our good works do.

SERMON 259, 4

SCRIPTURE

Put on, then, as God's chosen ones, holy and beloved, heart-felt compassion, kindness, humility, gentleness, and patience, bearing with one another and forgiving one another, if one has a grievance against another; as the Lord has forgiven you, so must you also do. And over all these put on love, that is, the bond of perfection. And let the peace of Christ control your hearts, the peace into which you were also called in one body. And be thankful....And whatever you do, in word or in deed, do everything in the name of the Lord Jesus, giving thanks to God the Father through him.

COLOSSIANS 3:12–15, 17

PRAYER

Loving Lord Jesus, today your Church leads us in a prayer of gladness: *Laetare! Rejoice!* The Lenten season has reached a mid-mark, and we are given this pause to renew our commitment and energy to resume the journey, lest we falter on the way. May the action of your Holy Spirit in our lives lead us to reach out to encourage others to seek peace, to embrace others with love, to be kind in word and deed. Amen.

PRACTICE

Turn to the Lord Jesus and ask for forgiveness for the failings in your Lenten commitment as you reflect on his first fall beneath the weight of the cross.

DAY 27

MONDAY OF THE FOURTH WEEK OF LENT

Hearts Fixed Firmly in Faith

*T*his is the first commandment, this is the beginning of our religion and our journey, our road—to have our hearts fixed firmly in faith, and by fixing our hearts firmly in faith to live good lives, to abstain from seductive goods, to endure patiently temporal evils. And as long as the enticement of the first and the threats of the second persist, to keep our heart steady and unshaken against each of them, so that you don't sink into the former or break yourself on the latter.

SERMON 38, 5

SCRIPTURE

Out of the heavens he let you hear his voice to discipline you; on earth he let you see his great fire, and you heard him speaking out of the fire....This is why you must now acknowledge, and fix in your heart, that the LORD is God in the heavens above and on earth below, and that there is no other. And you must keep his statutes and commandments which I command you today, that you and your children after you may prosper, and that you may have long life on the land which the LORD, your God, is giving you forever.

DEUTERONOMY 4:36, 39–40

PRAYER

Merciful Jesus, in the midst of the trials you had to face in life, you could always count on the love and understanding of your Blessed Mother, Mary. She was there on the road to Calvary, sharing your suffering, reminding you of her faithful embrace with you of the Father's will. Let me remember that your Mother is also my mother, a sure refuge in every difficult moment of life. Let me trust her and love her as you did. Amen.

PRACTICE

Take time to reflect on the ones you have loved and suffered with in the name of inner freedom to fulfill the will of God.

DAY 28

His Mercy Endures Forever

good man deposits in the heavenly bank all the works of mercy he does for the people he helps, and he knows that the one who keeps his deposit safe is the faithful and reliable guardian. He doesn't see it, but he is certain of his account, because nothing can be pilfered from it by a thief, or seized by an invading enemy, or taken away from him as though he were being evicted by a rival or bully or strong man, but it will always be waiting for him because it is being kept for him by the mightiest Lord of all.

SERMON 18, 3

SCRIPTURE

Praise the LORD, for he is good; for his mercy endures forever;
Praise the God of gods, for his mercy endures forever
Praise the Lord of lords; for his mercy endures forever...
The Lord remembered us in our low estate,
* for his mercy endures forever;*
Freed us from our foes, for his mercy endures forever;
And gives bread to all flesh, for his mercy endures forever.
Praise the God of heaven, for his mercy endures forever.

PSALM 136:1–3, 23–26

PRAYER

Merciful, all-loving Father, I can never come to the end when I try to count the manifold blessings I have received from you, for myself as well as for those dear to me. I pray that you be as generous in your goodness to all those persons who are in want, because of the thoughtlessness and greed of others. Let my eyes be open to see the need of those around me and to reach out and share. Amen.

PRACTICE

Jesus looked at Simon the Cyrenian and knew it is sometimes more blessed to receive than to give. When did you last say, "Thank you?"

WEDNESDAY OF THE FOURTH WEEK OF LENT

How Do We Know God?

*H*ow do we know God? From the things God made. Question the beauty of the earth, question the beauty of the sea, question the beauty of the air simply spread around everywhere, question the beauty of the sky, question the serried ranks of the stars, question the sun making the day glorious with its bright beams, question the moon tempering the darkness of the following night with its shining rays, question the animals that move in the waters, that amble about on dry land, that fly in the air...question all these things. They all answer you, "Here we are; look, we're beautiful."

SERMON 241, 2

SCRIPTURE

Now will I recall God's works; what I have seen, I will describe. ...*As the shining sun is clear to all, so the glory of the LORD fills all his works; yet even God's holy ones must fail in recounting the wonders of the LORD, though God has given his hosts the strength to stand firm before his glory....How beautiful are all his works, delightful to gaze upon and a joy to behold! Everything lives and abides forever; and to meet each need all things are preserved. All of them differ, one from another, yet none of them has he made in vain; for each in turn, as it comes, is good; can one ever see enough of their splendor?*

SIRACH 42:15, 16–17, 22–25

PRAYER

Blessed Jesus, when you met the holy woman Veronica on the way to Calvary, you marked her love and gentle care with a reward she could never have expected. As we reflect on the Sixth Station of the Cross, we pray for the grace to behold the beauty of your countenance in every face and one day see the splendor of the glory of God shining in your sacred face, O Christ! Amen.

PRACTICE

Wipe away the sweat, blood, and tears of the sacred face of Christ. Allow him to look within your heart and see his divine beauty reflected there.

DAY 30

You Will Harvest What You Have Sown

*I*f any aspect of this passing life is disturbing you, you should be all the more mindful to turn your thoughts to that life in which you will live with nothing to trouble you. There you will not be escaping the irritating hardships of this short period of time but the terrible pain of everlasting fire. If now you strive with so much anxiety and attention and effort to keep from meeting some passing suffering, how much more solicitous should you be to escape the misery that lasts forever....Think on these things, and do not be backward in doing good works. In due time you will harvest what you have sown.

TO THE CLERGY AND PEOPLE OF HIPPO

SCRIPTURE

His disciples approached him and said, "Explain to us the parable of the weeds in the field." He said in reply, "He who sows good seed is the Son of Man, the field is the world, the good seed the children of the kingdom. The weeds are the children of the evil one, and the enemy who sows them is the devil. The harvest is the end of the age, and the harvesters are angels. Just as weeds are collected and burned [up] with fire, so will it be at the end of the age. The Son of Man will send his angels, and they will collect out of his kingdom all who cause others to sin and all evildoers....Then the righteous will shine like the sun in the kingdom of their Father."

MATTHEW 13:41, 43

PRAYER

All-powerful God, Scripture tells us that *life on earth is a warfare.* Indeed, the challenges we face daily in our struggles to be faithful in discipleship and persevere in this Lenten journey in spite of shattered dreams and inner emptiness only confirm the repeated refrains that exhaust us. Help me not to avoid your will in my life. Help me to look to Jesus, who falls a second time and, once again, rises to continue the way to the cross.

PRACTICE

Draw on the strength of the suffering Christ to face what it is that God asks of you in accepting life not as a problem, but as a mystery.

DAY 31

Do More

I've been told that you have forgotten your practice of providing clothing for the poor. I urged this work of mercy on you when I was with you, and urge it on you now, so that you will not be overcome and made slothful by the destruction of this world. The things you see happening are just those that our Lord and Redeemer, who cannot lie, foretold would come. This is not the time to do fewer works of mercy, but, rather, more than you have been accustomed to do. So should Christians...transfer unwearyingly and with all speed the goods they were intending to store up on earth to the treasure house of heaven.

TO THE CLERGY AND PEOPLE OF HIPPO

SCRIPTURE

"Come, you who are blessed by my Father. Inherit the kingdom prepared for you from the foundation of the world. For I was hungry and you gave me food, I was thirsty and you gave me drink, a stranger and you welcomed me, naked and you clothed me, ill and you cared for me, in prison and you visited me.... Amen, I say to you, whatever you did for one of these least brothers of mine, you did for me."

MATTHEW 25:34–36, 40

PRAYER

Beautiful Lord Jesus, as you looked with love on the women weeping for you along the way to Calvary, you reached out to teach them to shed their tears for themselves and their children. So too, you ask us to answer your call to become humble by bearing fruits of compassion, forgiveness, gentleness, and healing for ourselves and others. May it be so. Amen.

PRACTICE

Be patient today with someone who appeals to you for support in a trying situation.

DAY 32

From Pride to Humility

We humans had first to be brought down from the unreal height of pride to humility, so that we could rise from there and acquire a real exaltation. For us to have this spirit, the more glorious for its very gentleness, communicated to us, so that our vehemence could be subdued by persuasion and not by force, would have been impossible for us unless the Word...condescended to act out his role and reveal himself in human form, so that we humans would be more afraid of being raised up by human arrogance than of being humbled by God's example.

TO THE PEOPLE OF MADAURA

SCRIPTURE

"God resists the proud, but gives grace to the humble." So submit yourselves to God. Resist the devil, and he will flee from you. Draw near to God, and he will draw near to you. Cleanse your hands, you sinners, and purify your hearts, you of two minds. Begin to lament, to mourn, to weep. Let your laughter be turned into mourning and your joy into dejection. Humble yourselves before the Lord and he will exalt you.

JAMES 4:6–10

PRAYER

Most Holy God, I see your beloved Son fall again beneath the weight of the cross, too heavy with our offenses, even with the help of Simon. What were the thoughts of that man, forced into a role of service he did not seek? Surely he was touched by grace as he walked by the side of this silent, suffering man. The love in the heart of Jesus must have embraced this Cyrenian. Let it embrace me, also. Amen.

PRACTICE

Reflect on the mission entrusted to you by the Father. Ask for the grace to pick yourself up after every fall and carry your cross.

DAY 33

THE FIFTH SUNDAY OF LENT

Be My Constant Guide

*I*n all our human affairs, then, we find no real pleasure unless we have a friend. But how many people do we find in this life about whose spirit and character we may feel perfectly secure? None of us is known to another person as we know ourselves; and yet neither do we know ourselves well enough to feel secure about our own behavior, even the very next day....In the darkness of this present life, in which we live as exiles from the Lord, walking as we do by faith and not by sight, a Christian heart should feel itself desolate so that it will not cease to pray.

TO PROBA, A WIDOW

SCRIPTURE

Therefore I prayed, and prudence was given me; I pleaded and the spirit of Wisdom came to me. I preferred her to scepter and throne, and deemed riches nothing in comparison with her, nor did I liken any priceless gem to her....Beyond health and beauty I loved her, and I chose to have her rather than the light, because her radiance never ceases. Yet all good things together came to me with her, and countless riches at her hands; I rejoiced in them all, because Wisdom is their leader.

WISDOM 7:7–9, 10–12

PRAYER

Holy Spirit of God, I stand before you, aware of the ways in which I have so foolishly boasted of my own righteousness. The light of your gift of wisdom enables me to see the errors of my ways, the failures of my resolutions, the distance between what I claim to be and what, in your sight, I am. Guide me along the right path as only you can. Once again, I begin anew to follow your direction. Be my constant guide. Amen.

PRACTICE

In a spirit of humility, recognize the ways in which you have so often failed to pursue the promises you have made to God. Begin today, as if for the first time, to live as you are called to do.

DAY 34

Is This All?

*O*ur welfare consists in life itself—in good health, and integrity of mind and body....And is this all? Is the summit of the happy life to be found in these things? Or does truth teach us that there is something else we are to prefer to them all? The sufficiency of what we need and our own welfare and that of our friends, as long as these belong only to this present time, must be cast aside for the sake of obtaining eternal life....Everything we can usefully and properly desire must certainly be seen in respect to the one life that is lived with God and that comes from God.

TO PROBA, A WIDOW

SCRIPTURE

The LORD gives wisdom,
from his mouth come knowledge and understanding;
He has success in store for the upright,
is the shield of those who walk honestly,
Guarding the paths of justice,
protecting the way of his faithful ones,
Then you will understand what is right and just,
what is fair, every good path;
For wisdom will enter your heart,
knowledge will be at home in your soul,
Discretion will watch over you,
understanding will guard you.

PROVERBS 2:6–11

PRAYER

Lord Jesus Christ, in the strength of your sacred passion, I hear your voice challenging me to follow you totally in a life of just faith, of practical love, of holy abandonment. Help me to know what it is in my life that will help me along this Lenten journey. Give me strength to set aside what will keep me from staying with you to the end and rejoice with your faithful disciples in the glory of your resurrection. Amen.

PRACTICE

Ask for the grace to be stripped of all that keeps you from becoming the little child Christ asks you to be. Do not fear the simplistic ridicule of those who have not heard the summons.

DAY 35

Let Your Requests Be Made Known to God

*T*his happy life is what we must always desire from the Lord our God, and what we must always pray for. At certain hours, though, we recall our minds from our other concerns and occupations, which in some measure cool our desire to the occupation of prayer. We admonish ourselves, by the words of our prayer, to fix our minds on what we desire; what has begun to cool may grow altogether cold and become extinct, unless it is frequently rekindled. The Apostle says, "Let your requests be made known to God."

TO PROBA, A WIDOW

SCRIPTURE

My [child], do not forget my teaching,
take to heart my commands;
For many days, and years of life,
and peace, will they bring you.
Do not let love and fidelity forsake you;
bind them around your neck;
write them on the tablet of your heart.
Then will you win favor and esteem
before God and human beings.
Trust in the LORD with all your heart,
on your own intelligence do not rely;
In all your ways be mindful of him,
and he will make straight your paths.

PROVERBS 3:1–6

PRAYER

Merciful God, with the infinite love of your Fatherly heart, you looked on your beloved Son as he was being nailed to the cross. His love led him to do your will to the very end. I thank you for this inestimable gift, even as I thank Jesus for the total surrender of himself given for me. Let me begin to give something of myself, every day, for the glory of your name and the triumph of the cross in the world. Amen.

PRACTICE

Reflect on the total sacrifice of Jesus, given that you may live your life so that it is not in vain.

DAY 36

You Will Not Lack Opportunities

*I*s there anything that the Lord God gives to people that he doesn't give from compassion, when even tribulation is his gift? Good fortune is his gift when he is encouraging us, and ill fortune is his gift when he is warning us. If, as I've said, he gives these even to the wicked, what is he preparing for those who wait for him? Be happy that his grace has made you one of these, forbearing one another in love, being eager to maintain the unity of the Spirit in the bond of peace. You will not lack opportunities of bearing with one another until the Lord has so purified you that God may be all in all.

TO THE NUNS OF HIPPO

SCRIPTURE

As long as the heir is not of age, he is no different from a slave, although he is the owner of everything, but he is under the supervision of guardians and administrators until the date set by his father. In the same way we also, when we were not of age, were enslaved to the elemental powers of the world. But when the fullness of time had come, God sent his Son, born of a woman, born under the law, to ransom those under the law, so that we might receive adoption. As proof that you are children, God sent the spirit of his Son into our hearts, crying out, "Abba, Father!"

GALATIANS 4:1–6

PRAYER

Eternal Father, your beloved Son cried out to you on the cross before surrendering his spirit into your hands. This is the same Son who once claimed, "I am not alone, because the Father is with me" (John 16:32). As Jesus died on the cross, he entered into the only rest he could ever know, union with you, his beloved *Abba*. May the triumph of the cross be the assurance we need as we seek to place all our trust in you. Amen.

PRACTICE

Spend time today in the presence of the Blessed Sacrament, offering with the dying Christ the prayer that was his: "Father, into your hands I commend my spirit" (Luke 23:46).

DAY 37

God Will Judge the World

I appeal to you...as St. Paul begged the Corinthians, by the name of our Lord Jesus Christ, that you all speak the same thing and that there be no divisions among you. First of all, the Lord Jesus (as St. John tells us in the Gospel) did not come to condemn the world, but that the world might be saved through him. And second, as St. Paul wrote, God will judge the world when he has come to judge the living and the dead....In the absence of grace, how does he save the world? And in the absence of free will, how will he judge it?

TO VALENTINUS AND THE MONKS OF HADRUMETUM

SCRIPTURE

But you, beloved, build yourselves up in your most holy faith; pray in the holy Spirit. Keep yourselves in the love of God and wait for the mercy of our Lord Jesus Christ that leads to eternal life. On those who waver, have mercy; save others by snatching them out of the fire; on others have mercy with fear....To the one who is able to keep you from stumbling and to present you unblemished and exultant, in the presence of his glory, to the only God, our savior, through Jesus Christ our Lord be glory, majesty, power, and authority from ages past, now, and for ages to come. Amen.

JUDE 1:20–25

PRAYER

Lord Jesus, I stand at the foot of the cross as your disciples take your body down and place it in the arms of your Blessed Mother. The prophecy of Simeon echoes in her ears as the sword of sorrow pierces her loving heart. Her *fiat* is one with yours as she accepts your final gift to her as our Mother. Receive my thanks for this gift and my commitment to your Father's will in my life. Amen.

PRACTICE

Accept the reality of the sorrow that may come as you strive to live the present moment with grace for whatever this day brings.

DAY 38

My Faith Makes Me Different

*W*ho makes you different from other people?"...God alone makes of a man or woman a vessel for noble and not for ignoble use. But because people who are unspiritual and filled up with empty pride may respond to [this] question, either in their thoughts or aloud, by saying: "My faith makes me different," or "My prayer," or "My righteousness," the Apostle immediately contests these thoughts and asks, "What have you that you did not receive? If then you received it, why do you glory as if it were not a gift?"

TO VALENTINUS AND THE MONKS OF HADRUMETUM

SCRIPTURE

What do you possess that you have not received? But if you have received it, why are you boasting as if you did not receive it? You are already satisfied; you have already grown rich; you have become kings without us! Indeed, I wish that you had become kings, so that we also might become kings with you....I am writing you this not to shame you, but to admonish you as my beloved children....Therefore, I urge you, be imitators of me.... For the kingdom of God is not a matter of talk but of power.

1 CORINTHIANS 4:7–8, 14, 16, 20

PRAYER

Gracious and generous God, you have given us your Son, Jesus Christ, and with him you have given us all things. How often I act as if your gifts were totally mine, of my own making and design! How often I forget that what I have is priceless only because it has come from you and is entrusted to me for the good of others. Open my eyes to the truth that you call me to live. Amen.

PRACTICE

Let your mantra today be, "Jesus meek and lowly of heart, make my heart like yours!"

SATURDAY OF THE FIFTH WEEK OF LENT

Pray Earnestly

*N*ow we will see whether you are a courageous man or not: conquer the cravings with which you love the world, and repent of your past...when those cravings overcame you....If you take this advice, if you hold on to it and keep it, you will obtain reliable blessings, and also live among those who are unreliable without harm to your soul....Pray earnestly; and say to God, in the words of the psalm, "Set me free from my troubles!" God answered your prayers...for deliverance from the many grave dangers connected with your visible, physical battles....The same God will answer your prayers for an invisible and spiritual victory over your inner, invisible enemies, your cravings themselves.

TO BONIFACE, COUNT OF AFRICA

SCRIPTURE

Thanks be to God who gives us the victory through our Lord Jesus Christ. Therefore, my beloved, be firm, steadfast, always fully devoted to the work of the Lord, knowing that in the Lord your labor is not in vain....Be on your guard, stand firm in the faith, be courageous, be strong. Your every act should be done with love....If anyone does not love the Lord, let him be accursed. Marana tha. The grace of the Lord Jesus be with you. My love to all of you in Christ Jesus.

1 CORINTHIANS 15:57–58; 16:13–14, 22–24

PRAYER

Merciful God, as our Lenten journey draws to a close, I thank you for the graces you have blessed me with through the challenges of the past weeks. Without the presence of your love, I would so often have strayed from the path to which I had committed myself. In the strength of the passion and peace that flows from your Son's fidelity to your will, I renew my resolve, with the help of thy merciful, abundant redemption. Amen.

PRACTICE

Spend time today with Christ as he prepares to enter the city of Jerusalem to begin this final week of his journey to Calvary.

DAY 40

PALM SUNDAY

Partakers in His Divinity

The only thing to cleanse the wicked and the proud is the blood of the just man and the humility of God; to contemplate God, which by nature we are not, we would have to be cleansed by him who became what by nature we are and what by sin we are not. By nature we are not God; by nature we are men; by sin we are not just. So God became a just man to intercede with God for sinful man. The sinner did not match the just, but man did match man. So...becoming a partaker of our mortality he made us partakers of his divinity.

THE TRINITY, IV, 4

80

SCRIPTURE

He is the beginning, the firstborn from the dead, that in all things he himself might be preeminent. For in him all the fullness was pleased to dwell, and through him to reconcile all things for him, making peace by the blood of his cross....And you who once were alienated and hostile in mind because of evil deeds he has now reconciled in his fleshly body through his death, to present you holy, without blemish, and irreproachable before him, provided that you persevere in the faith, firmly grounded, stable, and not shifting from the hope of the gospel that you heard.

COLOSSIANS 1:18–23

PRAYER

Loving Lord Jesus, today, with believers throughout the world, I sing, "Hosanna in the highest. Blessed is he who comes in the name of the Lord. Hosanna in the highest." Yes, Lord, you are indeed King of Israel and of all the world. Let me so live during the coming week not as those who turn their hearts from you at the slightest sign of trouble or rejection or persecution, but give me the grace to be faithful to you until the end. Amen.

PRACTICE

Recall frequently during the day the song of all those who celebrate the entry of Jesus into Jerusalem: Hosanna!

DAY 41

Love That Love

*L*et no one say, "I don't know what to love." Let him love his brother, and love that love....There now, he can already have God better known to him than his brother, certainly better known because more present, better known because more inward to him, better known because more sure. Embrace love which is God and embrace God with love. This is the love which unites all the good angels and all the servants of God in a bond of holiness....The more we are cured of the tumor of pride, the fuller we are of love. And if a man is full of love, what is he full of but God?

THE TRINITY, VI

SCRIPTURE

Beloved, let us love one another, because love is of God; everyone who loves is begotten by God and knows God. Whoever is without love does not know God, for God is love. In this way the love of God was revealed to us: God sent his only Son into the world so that we might have life through him. In this is love: not that we have loved God, but that he loved us and sent his Son as expiation for our sins. Beloved, if God so loved us, we also must love one another. No one has ever seen God. Yet, if we love one another, God remains in us, and his love is brought to perfection in us.

1 JOHN 4:7–12

PRAYER

Gentle Lord Jesus, today I remember that you had cherished friends on earth, among them the family in Bethany: Martha, Mary, and Lazarus. I thank you for the gift you have given me in dear friends through whom and with whom I have come to know you better, to love you more deeply, to serve you more faithfully. Because of them, I am able, with you and through you, to love your Father and your Spirit of love. Thank you for these gifts. Amen.

PRACTICE

Reflect today on the way in which you try to prove yourself to someone who has been given to you by the Lord to share your journey through life in holy friendship.

DAY 42

Cling to God

*J*ust as a snake does not walk with open stride but wriggles along by the tiny movements of its scales, so the careless glide little by little along the slippery path of failure, and beginning from a distorted appetite for being like God, they end up becoming like beasts....For man's true honor is God's image and likeness in him, but it can only be preserved when facing him from whom its impression is received. And so the less love he has for what is his very own, the more closely can he cling to God.

THE TRINITY, XII, 16

SCRIPTURE

Now the Lord is the Spirit, and where the Spirit of the Lord is, there is freedom. All of us, gazing with unveiled face on the glory of the Lord, are being transformed into the same image from glory to glory, as from the Lord who is the Spirit. Therefore, since we have this ministry through the mercy shown us, we are not discouraged. Rather, we have renounced shameful, hidden things; not acting deceitfully or falsifying the word of God, but by the open declaration of the truth we commend ourselves to everyone's conscience in the sight of God.

2 CORINTHIANS 3:17—4:2

PRAYER

Dear God, in this holiest of all weeks in the Church year, I renew my commitment of fidelity to the Christian life and the call to be a disciple of your Son, Jesus Christ. I do not count on my own strength of soul to be faithful. I know my own frailty in facing temptations of every sort. I pray for the gift of fortitude, promised by your Holy Spirit, to persevere in the way to which I have been called. Amen.

PRACTICE

Plan for your Easter sacrament of reconciliation through a sincere examination of conscience.

DAY 43

From This Life to the Happy Life

*T*he faith by which we believe in God is particularly necessary in this mortal life, so full of delusion and distress and
uncertainty. God is the only source to be found of any good things,
but especially of those which make a man good and those which
will make him happy; only from him do they come into a man and
attach themselves to a man. And only when a man who is faithful
and good in these unhappy conditions passes from this life to the
happy life will there really and truly be what now cannot possibly
be, namely, that a man lives as he would.

THE TRINITY, XIII, 10

SCRIPTURE

Therefore, since we have been justified by faith, we have peace with God through our Lord Jesus Christ, through whom we have gained access [by faith] to this grace in which we stand, and we boast in hope of the glory of God. Not only that, but we even boast of our afflictions, knowing that affliction produces endurance, and endurance, proven character, and proven character, hope, and hope does not disappoint, because the love of God has been poured out into our hearts through the holy Spirit that has been given to us.

ROMANS 5:1–5

PRAYER

Jesus, Savior of the world, this day is often called Spy Wednesday, as your betrayal by Judas Iscariot is remembered by those of us who seek to support you in your journey to Calvary. We pray for the grace to resist the temptation to despair of your mission, as we look around us at a world that seems not to change despite your promises to bring all peoples to you. Grant us the grace to stay with you to the end. Amen.

PRACTICE

Pray for the conversion of sinners who have been members of the Church since early childhood.

DAY 44

You Are What You Receive

*T*he bread which you can see on the altar, sanctified by the word of God, is the Body of Christ. That cup, or rather what the cup contains, sanctified by the word of God, is the Blood of Christ. It was by means of these things that the Lord Christ wished to present us with his Body and Blood, which he shed for our sake for the forgiveness of sins. If you receive them well, you are yourselves what you receive.

SERMON 227

SCRIPTURE

When the hour came, he took his place at table with the apostles. He said to them, "I have eagerly desired to eat this Passover with you before I suffer, for, I tell you, I shall not eat it [again] until there is fulfillment in the kingdom of God." Then he took a cup, gave thanks, and said, "Take this and share it among yourselves; for I tell you [that] from this time on I shall not drink of the fruit of the vine until the kingdom of God comes." Then he took the bread, said the blessing, broke it, and gave it to them, saying, "This is my body, which will be given for you; do this in memory of me." And likewise the cup after they had eaten, saying, "This cup is the new covenant in my blood, which will be shed for you."

LUKE 22:14–20

PRAYER

Jesus in the Blessed Sacrament, be praised, loved, adored, and thanked! This is the day to be grateful for the gift of the Holy Eucharist and of the priesthood of those called in your Church to share the grace that you, Eternal High Priest, have been given by your Father. Preserve and guard all those who have answered your call to ordained ministry. Grant to us who share baptismal priesthood the grace to know how to serve you. Amen.

PRACTICE

Take time today to renew your baptismal promises in the presence of Jesus in the Blessed Sacrament.

We Carry the Sign

*C*hrist's deformity is what gives form to you. If he had been unwilling to be deformed, you would never have gotten back the form you lost. So he hung on the cross, deformed, but his deformity was our beauty. In this life, let us hold on tight to the deformed Christ. *Far be it from me to boast, except in the cross of our Lord Jesus Christ, through whom the world has been crucified to me, and I to the world.* That's the deformity of Christ....We carry the sign of this deformity on our foreheads. Let us not be ashamed of this deformity of Christ.

SERMON 27, 6

SCRIPTURE

As they led him away they took hold of a certain Simon, a Cyrenian, who was coming in from the country; and after laying the cross on him, they made him carry it behind Jesus. A large crowd of people followed Jesus, including many women who mourned and lamented him. Jesus turned to them and said, "Daughters of Jerusalem, do not weep for me; weep instead for yourselves and for your children....Now two others, both criminals, were led away with him to be executed. When they came to the place called the Skull, they crucified him and the criminals there, one on his right, the other on his left. [Then Jesus said, "Father, forgive them, they know not what they do."]

LUKE 23:26–28, 32–34

PRAYER

Gracious Lord Jesus, did Simon the Cyrenian realize the privilege that was his in being chosen—forced, we could say—to help you carry your cross? As I reflect on what I count as the crosses I have to bear in my life, grant me the grace to know that each one allows me to share the burden of your suffering. Let me fill up in my body what is lacking in the weight you carried with Simon to Calvary. Amen.

PRACTICE

Take time today to make the Way of the Cross. If possible, spend the hours between noon and three o'clock in prayer, united to Jesus on the cross.

DAY 46

Our Hope...Our Faith...Our Charity

*T*he resurrection of the dead is our hope; the resurrection of the dead is our faith. It is also our charity, which blazes up at the proclamation of things that cannot yet be seen, and grows hot with a desire so huge that it gives our hearts the capacity to receive the bliss which is promised us for the future, enlarging them as long as they believe what they cannot yet see....And so take away faith in the resurrection of the dead, and the whole of Christian doctrine collapses.

SERMON 361, 2

SCRIPTURE

Now there was a virtuous and righteous man named Joseph who, though he was a member of the council, had not consented to their plan of action. He came from the Jewish town of Arimathea and was awaiting the kingdom of God. He went to Pilate and asked for the body of Jesus. After he had taken the body down, he wrapped it in a linen cloth and laid him in a rock-hewn tomb in which no one had yet been buried. It was the day of preparation, and the sabbath was about to begin. The women who had come from Galilee with him followed behind, and when they had seen the tomb and the way in which his body was laid in it, they returned and prepared spices and perfumed oils. Then they rested on the sabbath according to the commandment.

LUKE 23:50–56

PRAYER

Lord Jesus Christ, today more than on any other day in the year, let me spend the time close to the tomb where you have been buried. With the faith that is the gift of your Spirit, I pray for the grace to trust in the promises you have made as you foretold your passion, death, and resurrection. With your Mother, our Lady of Holy Saturday, I seek to embrace the meaning of your tomb. Amen.

PRACTICE

If possible, spend this day as a time of retreat and silence in watch at the tomb of the buried Christ.

PART II

~~~~~~~

READINGS

for

EASTER

DAY 47

EASTER SUNDAY

Jesus Christ Is the New Life

*T*he resurrection of our Lord Jesus Christ is the new life of those who believe in Jesus. And this is the mysterious meaning of his passion and resurrection, which you certainly ought to know about and live up to. It was not, after all, without reason that life came to death, not without reason that the fountain of life, from which one drinks to live, drank here the cup which was not his due. Dying, I mean, was not Christ's due. Where death came from—if we look for its origin, the father of death is sin. You see, if there had never been any sin, nobody would ever have died.

SERMON 231, 2

SCRIPTURE

After the sabbath, as the first day of the week was dawning, Mary Magdalene and the other Mary came to see the tomb. And behold, there was a great earthquake; for an angel of the Lord descended from heaven, approached, rolled back the stone, and sat upon it....The guards were shaken with fear of him and became like dead men. Then the angel said to the women in reply, "Do not be afraid! I know that you are seeking Jesus the crucified. He is not here, for he has been raised just as he said. Come and see the place where he lay. Then go quickly and tell his disciples, 'He has been raised from the dead, and he is going before you to Galilee; there you will see him.'"

MATTHEW 28:1–2, 4–7

PRAYER

Risen Lord, in praise of your glory, I unite my Easter song to that of your holy Mother, as she embraced you on that first glorious morning. She it was who welcomed you before anyone else. She it was whom you desired to see before any other person. Let me be glad because of her unsurpassed love for you and your unique love for her. Let the grace of your resurrection bring joy to my soul today. Amen.

PRACTICE

Let the heart of Mary find another voice in her alleluia song today as together with her you praise the risen Lord. Alleluia!

DAY 48

Joy in Hope

*I*t's in hope that we sing *alleluia.* Just look what joy there is in hope. What will the reality itself be like?...What, after all, is *alleluia,* my brothers and sisters? I've told you, it's the praise of God. There you are, you hear the word now, and hearing it you are delighted, and in your delight you are praising him....After all, if we praise what we believe, how are we going to praise when we see? There you have the part that Mary chose for herself; but she was representing that life, not yet possessing it.

SERMON 255, 5

SCRIPTURE

Shout joyfully to the LORD, all you lands;
serve the LORD with gladness;
come before him with joyful song.
Know that the LORD is God,
he made us, we belong to him,
we are his people, the flock he shepherds.
Enter his gates with thanksgiving,
his courts with praise.
Give thanks to him, bless his name;
good indeed is the LORD,
His mercy endures forever,
his faithfulness lasts through every generation.

PSALM 100

PRAYER

Spirit of God, open my eyes to see how and where and how frequently the risen Lord appears to me in these days following his resurrection. Let me not be surprised by the unexpected sightings of my glorious Lord and Savior in the most humble places, but let me proclaim everywhere and always: Christ is risen! He is truly risen! Alleluia! Amen.

PRACTICE

Let the joy of the resurrection so fill your heart that it becomes contagious in the soul of everyone you meet.

He Opened Their Minds

*A*fter his resurrection, Christ showed himself to his disciples, he indicated his scars, presenting them to be handled and felt, as well as to be seen. They, however, while holding him, and touching and recognizing him, still for all that hesitated for sheer joy, as the gospel tells us, and not to believe that is impious. But while they were still hesitating and doubting for joy, the Lord brought some definite certainty into the situation from the Scriptures....*I told you this while I was still with you.*...Then he opened their minds to understand the Scriptures.

SERMON 162A, 10

SCRIPTURE

Now that very day two of them were going to a village...called Emmaus, and they were conversing about all the things that had occurred....Jesus himself drew near and walked with them, but their eyes were prevented from recognizing him. He asked, "What are you discussing as you walk along?"...One of them... said to him in reply, "Are you the only visitor to Jerusalem who does not know of the things that have taken place there in these days?...The things that happened to Jesus the Nazarene?"... And he said to them,..."Was it not necessary that the Messiah should suffer these things and enter into his glory?"...While he was with them at table, he took bread, said the blessing, broke it, and gave it to them. With that their eyes were opened.

LUKE 24:13–19, 25–26, 30–31

PRAYER

Dearest Lord, let me not be led astray by the doubts of the age in which I live, as people scoff at what faith in the risen Christ leads to. Strengthen my faith to become a shining light to sustain the wavering struggles of others. Send your Holy Spirit to open the eyes of my mind to understand the words of Scripture. Give me the words to help others see and believe, with the help of your grace. Amen.

PRACTICE

During these Easter days, as I read the scriptural accounts of the Lord's appearances to his disciples, let me reflect in faith and gratitude on the power of the resurrection in my life.

DAY 50

Let Alleluia Be Sung

*E*ven here, among the dangers, among the trials and temptations of this life both by others and by us, let *alleluia* be sung. God is faithful...who will not permit you to be tempted beyond what you are able to endure. So here too let us sing *alleluia*....He didn't say he will not permit you to be tempted, but *will not permit you to be tempted beyond what you are able to endure*....But when you enter the temptation, bear in mind the way out; because God is faithful, *God will watch over your going in and your coming out.*

SERMON 256, 3

SCRIPTURE

Thomas, called Didymus, one of the Twelve, was not with them when Jesus came. So the other disciples said to him, "We have seen the Lord." But he said to them, "Unless I see the mark of the nails in his hands and put my finger into the nailmarks and put my hand into his side, I will not believe." Now a week later his disciples were again inside and Thomas was with them. Jesus came, although the doors were locked, and stood in their midst and said, "Peace be with you." Then he said to Thomas, "Put your finger here and see my hands, and bring your hand and put it into my side, and do not be unbelieving, but believe." Thomas answered and said to him, "My Lord and my God!" Jesus said to him, "...Blessed are those who have not seen and have believed."

JOHN 20:24–29

PRAYER

Holy God, mighty God, immortal God! In the resurrection of Jesus Christ, the promise of our redemption has been fully realized. With Thomas, let me be not unbelieving but grateful for the grace and power that is mine as I proclaim with believers everywhere, "My Lord and my God!" Let my faith be strengthened through contemplation of the glorious wounds of Christ, signs of his triumph over sin and death. May the witness of my belief speak to others. Amen.

PRACTICE

Today, let my prayer be that of the believing Thomas: "My Lord and my God!"

DAY 51

He Paid Our Price

*T*he glorification of our Lord Jesus Christ was completed by his rising again and ascending into heaven. The reason he rose again was to show us an example of resurrection, and the reason he ascended was to protect us from above. So we have our Lord and savior Jesus Christ first hanging on the tree, now seated in heaven. He paid our price when he was hanging on the tree; he has been gathering up what he bought while seated in heaven....He will come at the end of time, and it is written, *God will come openly*; not as he came the first time, disguised; but as it says, *openly*.

SERMON 263, 1

SCRIPTURE

Jesus revealed himself again to his disciples at the Sea of Tiberias....Simon Peter said to them, "I am going fishing." ...When it was already dawn, Jesus was standing on the shore; but the disciples did not realize that it was Jesus. Jesus said to them, "Children, have you caught anything to eat?" They answered him, "No." So he said to them, "Cast the net over the right side of the boat and you will find something." So they cast it, and were not able to pull it in because of the number of fish.... When they climbed out on shore, they saw a charcoal fire with fish on it and bread. Jesus said to them, "Bring some of the fish you just caught....Come, have breakfast." ...This was now the third time Jesus was revealed to his disciples after being raised from the dead.

JOHN 21:1–14

PRAYER

Risen, triumphant Lord, how unexpected your appearances to your disciples were after your resurrection! You went to them in the ordinary events of daily life. You reached out to them in the difficulties of daily activities. You called to them when they were least expecting it. Let me be attentive to watch for you, to recognize you, to respond to your gentle call. Let me find you as I seek you and seek you again when I have found you. Amen.

PRACTICE

Be alert today for the appearance of the risen Lord as you go about your daily duties so you may respond to his presence.

DAY 52

FRIDAY OF EASTER WEEK

I Can Hear You

My brothers and sisters, my children, O seedlings of the Catholic Church, O holy and heavenly seed, O you that have been born again in Christ and been born from above, listen to me—or rather, listen to God through me: *Sing to the Lord a new song.* "Well, I *am* singing," you say. Yes, you are singing, of course you're singing. I can hear you. But don't let your life give evidence against your tongue. Sing with your voices—sing also with your hearts; sing with your mouths—sing also with your conduct.

SERMON 34, 6

SCRIPTURE

For this reason I kneel before the Father, from whom every family in heaven and on earth is named, that he may grant you in accord with the riches of his glory to be strengthened with power through his Spirit in the inner self, and that Christ may dwell in your hearts through faith; that you, rooted and grounded in love, may have strength to comprehend with all the holy ones what is the breadth and length and height and depth, and to know the love of Christ that surpasses knowledge, so that you may be filled with all the fullness of God.

EPHESIANS 3:14–19

PRAYER

Dear Lord Jesus, the joy of your resurrection continues to echo throughout the world as your faithful people sing the Easter canticles that proclaim your gift to us of a new life and a new song. Let the music of our hearts rise with that of your entire Church to thank you for the graces you share with us. May the days ahead be blessed as we seek to join the company of all your saints who praise your endless mercy. Amen.

PRACTICE

Let gratitude be the theme song of your prayer today as you rejoice in the graces of the Lord's resurrection.

DAY 53

Follow the Lord

*F*ollow the Lord....Where he went, we know perfectly well; we solemnly celebrated that occasion only a very few days ago. He rose from the dead, he ascended into heaven; that's where we are to follow him to. Obviously we mustn't despair about getting there—but because he made us the promise, not because we mere human beings can manage it on our own. Heaven was a long, long way away from us before our head had gone up to heaven....So that's where we have to follow him....It's good to follow him there.

SERMON 96, 3

SCRIPTURE

So, as you received Christ Jesus the Lord, walk in him, rooted in him and built upon him and established in the faith as you were taught, abounding in thanksgiving....For in him dwells the whole fullness of the deity bodily, and you share in this fullness in him, who is the head of every principality and power. In him you were also circumcised with a circumcision not administered by hand, by stripping off the carnal body, with the circumcision of Christ. You were buried with him in baptism, in which you were also raised with him through faith in the power of God, who raised him from the dead.

COLOSSIANS 2:6–7, 9–12

PRAYER

Glorious and risen Lord, the mystery of your resurrection speaks to each of us, individually, to those of us gathered in communities of discipleship and in your Church. As you call us and send us forth, we realize that this mystery is meant for the entire world. In faith and love, we pray, "The Word was made flesh and dwelt among us!" "The Word has risen and sends us forth in the Spirit!" May we go forth in peace, joy, and hope. Amen.

PRACTICE

Identify one way in which you can fulfill the risen Lord's mandate to "go forth to proclaim the Good News."

DAY 54

Make Steady Progress
in Renewal of His Image

*T*o be sure...renewal does not happen in one moment of conversion, as the baptismal renewal by the forgiveness of all sins happens in a moment so that not even one tiny sin remains unforgiven. But it is one thing to throw off a fever, another to recover from the weakness the fever leaves behind....The first stage of the cure is to remove the cause of the debility, and this is done by pardoning all sins; the second stage is curing the debility itself, and this is done gradually by making steady progress in the renewal of this image.

THE TRINITY, XIV, 23

SCRIPTURE

If then you were raised with Christ, seek what is above, where Christ is seated at the right hand of God. Think of what is above, not of what is on earth. For you have died, and your life is hidden with Christ in God. When Christ your life appears, then you too will appear with him in glory....Persevere in prayer, being watchful in it with thanksgiving....Conduct yourselves wisely toward outsiders, making the most of the opportunity. Let your speech always be gracious, seasoned with salt, so that you know how you should respond to each one.

COLOSSIANS 3:1–4; 4:2, 5–6

PRAYER

Holy Spirit of God, you are the advocate promised by the risen Lord before he ascended to his Father and ours. We turn to you, hoping for the light, the life, and the love that we know you can bring to us as we continue to rejoice in the remaining days of this Easter season. Prepare us for your coming in fire and flame; fill us with zeal to proclaim the fullness of truth that you will teach us. Come, Holy Spirit, come! Amen.

PRACTICE

Begin, even now, your prayer to the apostolic spirit of Jesus in preparation for the great feast of Pentecost.

Sources and Acknowledgments

Augustine Day by Day II: Daily Readings From the Sermons of St. Augustine, compiled and edited by John E. Rotelle, OSA, Augustinian Press, 1995.

Letters of St. Augustine, edited by John Leinenweber, Triumph Books, Tarrytown, NY, 1992.

The Trinity by St. Augustine; introduction, translation, and notes by Edmund Hill, OP; edited by John E. Rotelle, OSA; New City Press; Brooklyn, NY; Augustinian Heritage Institute; 1991.

Sermons to the People, translated and edited by William Griffin, Image Books, Doubleday, New York, 2002.

The Monastic Rules; The Augustine Series, Volume IV, New City Press, Hyde Park, NY, 2004.

The Four Volume Liturgy of the Hours, Volume IV, Catholic Book Publishing Co., New York, 1975.

CPSIA information can be obtained
at www.ICGtesting.com
Printed in the USA
FFOW05n1944250214

9 780764 820311